EYEWITNESS TO HISTORY

MAJOR CULTURAL MOVEMENTS

Inside the

ENVIRONMENTAL MOVEMENT

TRY RECYC

CLEAN AIR INSIDE F OUT

Gareth Stevens
PUBLISHING

By Janey Levy

Please visit our website, www.garethstevens.com. For a free color catalog of all our high-quality books, call toll free 1-800-542-2595 or fax 1-877-542-2596.

Library of Congress Cataloging-in-Publication Data

Names: Levy, Janey, author.
Title: Inside the environmental movement / Janey Levy.
Description: New York : Gareth Stevens Publishing, 2018. | Series: Eyewitness to history: major cultural movements | Includes index.
Identifiers: LCCN 2017028769| ISBN 9781538211571 (pbk.) | ISBN 9781538211588 (6 pack) | ISBN 9781538211595 (library bound)
Subjects: LCSH: Environmentalism–United States–History–Juvenile literature. | Environmentalists–United States–Biography–Juvenile literature. | Environmental protection–United States–History–Juvenile literature.
Classification: LCC GE195.5 .L48 2018 | DDC 363.700973–dc23
LC record available athttps://lccn.loc.gov/2017028769

First Edition

Published in 2018 by
Gareth Stevens Publishing
111 East 14th Street, Suite 349
New York, NY 10003

Copyright © 2018 Gareth Stevens Publishing

Designer: Katelyn E. Reynolds
Editor: Therese Shea

Photo credits: Cover, pp. 1 (woman), 15, 17 Bettmann/Wikipedia.com; cover, p. 1 (background image) Anthony Pescatore/NY Daily News Archive via Getty Images; p. 1 (logo quill icon) Seamartini Graphics Media/Shutterstock.com; cover, p. 1 (logo stamp) YasnaTen/Shutterstock.com; cover, p. 1 (color grunge frame) DmitryPrudnichenko/Shutterstock.com; cover, pp. 1–32 (paper background) Nella/Shutterstock.com; cover, pp. 1–32 (decorative elements) Ozerina Anna/Shutterstock.com; pp. 1–32 (wood texture) Reinhold Leitner/Shutterstock.com; pp. 1–32 (open book background) Elena Schweitzer/Shutterstock.com; pp. 1–32 (bookmark) Robert Adrian Hillman/Shutterstock.com; p. 5 The Print Collector/Print Collector/Getty Images; p. 7 (book) Library of Congress/Corbis/VCG via Getty Images; p. 7 (portrait) National Portrait Gallery, Washington, DC; p. 9 courtesy of the Library of Congress/Brian0918/Wikipedia.org; p. 11 Library of Congress/digital version by Science Faction/Getty Images; p. 13 VCG Wilson/Corbis via Getty Images; pp. 19, 21 Library of Congress/Corbis/VCG via Getty Images; p. 23 Kevin Fleming/Corbis via Getty Images; p. 25 Alfred Eisenstaedt/The LIFE PictureCollection/Getty Images; p. 27 Richard M. Nixon Presidential Library, Yorba Linda, CA.

Printed in the United States of America

CPSIA compliance information: Batch #CW18GS: For further information contact Gareth Stevens, New York, New York at 1-800-542-2595.

CONTENTS

*Words in the glossary appear in **bold** type
the first time they are used in the text.*

ENVIRONMENTAL *Crisis*

Imagine a world where people looked at skies filled with factory smoke and saw not pollution, but a sign of progress. That was the world of the Industrial Revolution. The Industrial Revolution began in Great Britain around 1760, then spread across Europe and finally to the United States. It's called a revolution because it changed people's lives enormously. An economy based on industry and machine manufacturing replaced one based on agriculture and hand manufacturing.

But these **technological** changes led to a huge increase in the use of **natural resources**. Forests were cut down, and fuels such as coal and oil were widely used. Air, rivers, and oceans became polluted. Fortunately, people began to realize a crisis threatened life on Earth. The **environmental** movement was born.

MORE TO KNOW

During the Industrial Revolution, oceans and rivers seemed unlimited in size. People wrongly believed they could dump enormous amounts of waste into them without causing harm.

Because of the Industrial Revolution, goods became cheaper to produce, and more people could afford to buy those goods. However, the cost was environmental damage.

URBANIZATION

As jobs became available in factories, people moved to cities. Villages such as Manchester, England, quickly grew into cities of hundreds of thousands. This urbanization, or growth of cities, contributed to pollution. People crowded together, and waste and trash piled up. Friedrich Engels recorded his observations of Manchester: *"The view from this bridge . . . is characteristic for the whole district. At the bottom flows . . . the Irk [River], a narrow, coal-black, foul-smelling stream, full of debris and refuse [rubbish]."*

EARLY *Voices*

DISAPPEARING PLANTS

Scientists used Thoreau's records of over 500 wildflowers to study the effects of **climate change**. They discovered 27 percent of these plant species are no longer growing in Concord, Massachusetts, and another 36 percent are rare. Plants are sensitive to temperature change, so the scientists blame the disappearance of the flowers on rising global temperatures. Scientist Richard Primack said that if Thoreau were alive today, he would *"be involved in the movement to reduce the greenhouse gases that are linked to climate change."*

One of the earliest voices raised in defense of the environment was that of Henry David Thoreau (1817–1862). Though he was largely ignored in his own day, many today consider him the father of the modern environmental movement. His best-known book is *Walden*, based on the journal he kept during 2 years spent living a simple life close to nature at Walden Pond in Massachusetts.

Thoreau recognized people are part of the natural environment, not separate from it, and rely on its health for their own survival. He knew if people continued to use up natural resources, the wilderness would be destroyed. Thoreau urged some land be set aside to remain forever wild. *"In Wildness is the preservation of the World,"* he wrote.

MORE TO KNOW

In reaction to deforestation around his Concord, Massachusetts, hometown, Thoreau proposed: *"Each town should have a park, or rather a primitive forest, of 500 or a thousand acres, where a stick should never be cut for fuel, a common possession forever, for instruction and recreation."*

Walden was first published in 1854. It has since been translated into almost every major language and is more widely read than any other 19th-century nonfiction book.

Another early figure considered critical to the foundation of the environmental movement was George Perkins Marsh (1801–1882). Marsh has been called the father of the American conservation movement.

Growing up in Vermont, Marsh saw firsthand how damage to one part of an ecosystem could harm the whole system. Cutting down mountain forests led to erosion, destruction of fish **habitats**, and loss of farmland fertility. In an 1847 speech to Vermont farmers, Marsh warned of the dangers of clearing forests.

Humans' effect on nature was the theme of Marsh's 1864 book, *Man and Nature*. Unlike those who saw people's mark on the natural world as progress, he saw them as plunderers. He warned they must become conservers or the environment would worsen.

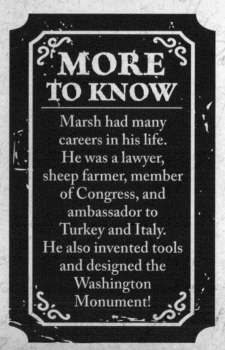

MORE TO KNOW

Marsh had many careers in his life. He was a lawyer, sheep farmer, member of Congress, and ambassador to Turkey and Italy. He also invented tools and designed the Washington Monument!

For Marsh, as for Thoreau, people were part of nature, not separate from it or above it. Marsh believed it was the duty of humankind to preserve natural resources for future generations.

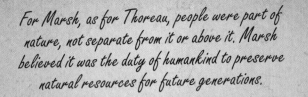

MAN AND NATURE

Marsh recognized all life on Earth is connected. Damage to one part would affect others, and humans lacked the knowledge and understanding to know how far the damage would spread: *"The Equation of animal and vegetable [plant] life is too complicated a problem for human intelligence to solve and we can never know how wide a circle of disturbance we produce in the harmonies of nature when we throw the smallest pebble into the ocean of organic life."*

9

JOHN MUIR
and the Sierra Club

NATURE OVER CIVILIZATION

Beginning in 1873, Muir wrote articles for leading magazines promoting his love of nature. These articles made Muir nationally famous. In an 1875 article, he observed that people seemed wrongly convinced they must always "improve" on nature: "*Nevertheless, the barbarous [ignorant] notion is almost universally entertained by civilized man, that there is in all the manufactures [creations] of Nature something essentially coarse which can and must be eradicated [destroyed] by human culture.*"

John Muir (1838–1914) was perhaps the best known of the environmental movement's early voices. He grew up in Wisconsin and attended college there, studying botany, or plant science, and geology. Arriving in California in 1868, John Muir fell in love with the Sierra Nevada, which he called "*the Range of Light . . . the most divinely beautiful of all the mountain chains I have ever seen.*"

Muir grew increasingly concerned about the damage to wilderness caused by human activities. He wrote, "*If the importance of our forests were at all understood . . . their preservation would call forth the most watchful attention of the government. . . . [yet] in many of the finest groves every species of destruction is still moving on with accelerated [hastened] speed.*"

10

MORE TO KNOW

Muir helped create Yosemite National Park in 1890 and other national parks as well, including Grand Canyon National Park. He's often called the Father of Our National Park System.

Muir was born in Scotland and moved to Wisconsin with his family in 1849.

In 1892, Muir and several of his supporters founded the Sierra Club. Its purpose, in Muir's words, was to *"do something for wildness and make the mountains glad."*

From the beginning, the club took action on environmental issues. It led an effort to defeat a proposed reduction of Yosemite National Park's boundaries in 1892. In 1897, the club urged strengthening public forest policy and supported proposals for additional "national forest parks." The next year, it established an office in Yosemite Valley to educate visitors. In 1905, the club succeeded in getting the California government to return Yosemite Valley to federal control, to be made part of Yosemite National Park. Muir served as the club's president until his death in 1914. Its work to fulfill his vision continues.

MORE TO KNOW

Muir had long urged the creation of a government office to oversee and protect the national parks. In 1916, President Woodrow Wilson signed an act creating the National Park Service.

Muir's well-loved Yosemite Valley is shown in this painting by Albert Bierstadt. Along with the writings of Muir and others, such works also helped inspire an appreciation of wild nature.

THE SIERRA CLUB TODAY

Today, the Sierra Club is the nation's largest environmental organization, with almost 3 million members and supporters. It has protected 250 million acres (100 million ha) of wilderness. It has also taken an active part in the fight to reduce pollution, which threatens civilization as well as wilderness. The Sierra Club helped promote the Clean Air Act (1963), Clean Water Act (1972), and Endangered Species Act (1973) and is now promoting a move to an economy based on **renewable energy**.

13

THEODORE
Roosevelt

Theodore Roosevelt (1858–1919) is known as America's first conservationist president. He was a naturalist, or student of the natural world, from the time he was a young boy. But he was also deeply influenced by John Muir and a camping trip he took with Muir in Yosemite in 1903. He said camping in Yosemite was *"like lying in a great solemn cathedral, far vaster and more beautiful than any built by the hand of man."*

Roosevelt was president from 1901 to 1909. During those years, he used his authority to issue **executive orders** that created 150 new national forests, protecting 172 million acres (70 million ha). He also created five national parks, 18 national monuments, and 51 wildlife refuges!

MORE TO KNOW

When Roosevelt was just 8 years old, he created his own nature museum, the Roosevelt Museum of Natural History. In 1871, he gave several of his specimens to the new American Museum of Natural History in New York City.

Muir helped Roosevelt (left) plan his conservation programs.

WILDLIFE
Conservationists

While many early environmentalists focused on aspects of the land such as forests, soil, and rivers, some were alarmed by what was happening to North American wildlife. Bison, which once roamed the plains in herds of millions, were nearly extinct by the late 1800s. Passenger pigeons, once the most abundant birds in North America, became extinct in 1914. William Hornaday (1854–1937) was one of the first to draw attention to **endangered** wildlife.

Hornaday worked tirelessly to protect wildlife. His books and articles helped bring about wildlife conservation laws. He helped keep the Alaskan fur seal from extinction by getting the 1911 North Pacific Fur Seal Treaty approved. He also helped the Migratory Bird Treaty Act to pass. But his biggest victory was saving the bison from extinction.

MORE TO KNOW

In 1913, Hornaday published a book titled *Our Vanishing Wildlife* to draw attention to the problem of endangered species.

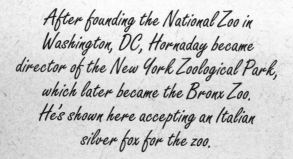

After founding the National Zoo in Washington, DC, Hornaday became director of the New York Zoological Park, which later became the Bronx Zoo. He's shown here accepting an Italian silver fox for the zoo.

SAVING THE BISON

In 1889, Hornaday published *The Extermination of the American Bison*, which created public support for saving the animal. He began the book with this comment: *"It is hoped that the following historical account of the . . . almost complete extermination [wiping out] of the great American bison may serve to cause the public to fully realize the folly of allowing all our most valuable and interesting American mammals to be wantonly [mercilessly] destroyed in the same manner."*

The man considered the father of wildlife conservation in the United States is Aldo Leopold (1887–1948). Leopold grew up in Iowa and joined the new US Forest Service in 1909, serving in Arizona and New Mexico.

In 1924, Leopold transferred to Wisconsin, where he taught at the University of Wisconsin in addition to his forest service duties. His 1933 book, *Game Management*, was the first textbook in the field of wildlife management and defined the skills for both managing and restoring wildlife populations. The book created a whole new field of science and led the university to create a new department, with Leopold as the head. Over the course of his life, Leopold published hundreds of articles in professional journals as well as popular magazines.

THE LAND ETHIC

One of Leopold's most influential ideas was the land ethic, which called for people to have a moral, caring relationship with the land. He explained the concept in *A Sand County Almanac*: *"All ethics so far evolved rest upon a single premise [idea]: that the individual is a member of a community of interdependent parts ... The land ethic simply enlarges the boundaries of the community to include soils, waters, plants, and animals, or collectively: the land."*

MORE TO KNOW

Leopold helped bring about the establishment of the Gila Wilderness in New Mexico in 1924. It was the first area in the world to be managed as a wilderness area. That means that human activities there are limited.

In 1935, Leopold helped found the Wilderness Society. He aided in founding the Wildlife Society the following year.

AMERICA'S
First Forester

Until the 1890s, no plan existed to manage US forests. Few people saw a need for one. Forests were seen as **inexhaustible**. Gifford Pinchot (1865–1946) changed Americans' way of thinking and introduced European science-based professional forestry. In 1896, Pinchot helped work out the plan for US forest reserves as a member of the National Forest Commission of the National Academy of Sciences. In 1898, he was named chief of the federal government's Division of Forestry. When the US Forest Service was created in 1905, he became its chief.

National forest land holdings increased from 56 million acres (23 million ha) to 172 million acres (70 million ha) during Pinchot's 5 years heading the US Forest Service. Pinchot also helped shape many of the conservation programs of his friend President Theodore Roosevelt.

MORE TO KNOW

Pinchot studied forestry in Europe because there were no schools for it in the United States. After he returned to the United States, he founded the Yale School of Forestry.

Few forestry jobs existed in the United States at the beginning of Pinchot's career. His first job was working at the Biltmore estate of George Vanderbilt in North Carolina.

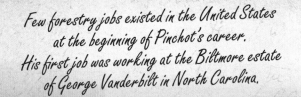

"TO WASTE TIMBER WAS A VIRTUE"

Pinchot related the situation he found in America when he returned from his European forestry studies: *"When I came home not a single acre of Government, state, or private timberland was under systematic forest management . . . To waste timber was a virtue and not a crime. . . . What talk there was about forest protection was no more to the average American than the buzzing of a mosquito, and just about as irritating."*

CHAMPION
of the Everglades

While most environmentalists of the time focused their efforts broadly, Marjory Stoneman Douglas (1890–1998) concentrated on the vast **wetland** ecosystem known as the Florida Everglades.

Douglas moved to Florida in 1915 and went to work with her father at the *Miami Herald* newspaper. People of the time generally saw wetlands such as the Everglades as useless and unattractive. But Douglas recognized the Everglades' importance as a source of freshwater for people and wildlife and wrote articles and books celebrating the wetland. She's most famous for her book *The Everglades: River of Grass*.

Douglas helped in the creation of Everglades National Park in 1947. She fought for the park the rest of her life and founded the group Friends of the Everglades around 1970.

MORE TO KNOW

In 1993, Douglas received the Presidential Medal of Freedom from President Bill Clinton for her work to protect the Everglades.

Douglas never stopped protecting the Everglades. After she died at the age of 108, she was cremated, and her ashes were scattered in Everglades National Park.

SILENT *Spring*

In 1962, a book appeared that's credited with giving the environmental movement new strength. That book was *Silent Spring*, and its author was Rachel Carson (1907–1964).

Carson became concerned with the dangers of chemical **pesticides**, especially the powerful DDT, while working at the US Fish and Wildlife Service. She left her job to work on *Silent Spring*. The book begins with an account of an imaginary town where spring is silent because pesticides have killed the birds and insects. She wrote, *"This town does not actually exist; I know of no community that has experienced all the misfortunes I describe. Yet every one of them has actually happened somewhere in the world."*

Silent Spring had a powerful effect. As a result of a national pesticide study, DDT was banned.

MORE TO KNOW

Pesticide companies attacked Carson after she published *Silent Spring*, but she stood by her work. She was also asked to talk before Congress.

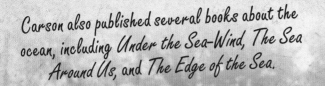

Carson also published several books about the ocean, including *Under the Sea-Wind*, *The Sea Around Us*, and *The Edge of the Sea*.

SILENT SPRING

Carson began *Silent Spring*: "The most alarming of all man's assaults upon the environment is the contamination of the air, earth, rivers, and seas with dangerous, and even lethal, materials. . . . Many man-made chemicals act in much the same way as radiation; they lie long in the soil, and enter into living organisms, passing from one to another. Or they may travel mysteriously by underground streams, emerging to . . . kill vegetation, sicken cattle, and work unknown harm on those who drink from once pure wells."

THE EPA

Over a century after Thoreau first raised his voice in defense of nature, the federal government finally took a big step in protecting the environment. In 1969, Congress passed the National Environmental Policy Act (NEPA), which made the government not only the conservator of wilderness, but also the protector of earth, air, land, and water.

In July 1970, President Richard Nixon informed Congress of his plan to create the Environmental Protection Agency (EPA). Since its creation, the EPA has been responsible for numerous laws that protect our air, land, and water from pollution and protect wildlife. Some of the best known are the Clean Water Act (1972) and Endangered Species Act (1973).

MORE TO KNOW

The worst oil spill in history was the Gulf of Mexico oil spill of 2010. An explosion aboard the Deepwater Horizon oil rig led to more than 205 million gallons (776 million L) of oil leaking into the gulf.

The first head of the EPA, William D. Ruckelshaus, said, "Each of us must begin to measure the impact of our own decisions and actions on the quality of air, water, and soil of this nation." He's shown below being sworn into his position.

ENVIRONMENTALISM
Today

MORE TO KNOW

The first Earth Day, an event to get people to focus on the environment, was held on April 22, 1970. It's been held every year on April 22 since then.

Today, environmentalism is advanced largely by **nonprofit** organizations. The Sierra Club remains active and influential. Other notable organizations include the Nature Conservancy, the World Wildlife Fund (also known as the World Wide Fund for Nature), and Greenpeace. These organizations work around the world to protect natural areas and wildlife and expose environmental problems.

After years of talks, nearly 200 nations took steps together to protect the environment with the Paris Climate Accord of 2015. They pledged to fight climate change by using renewable energy and reducing greenhouse gas emissions. However, on June 1, 2017, President Trump announced plans for the United States to withdraw from the agreement. Despite this decision, environmentalists and world leaders continue their efforts to fight climate change. The battle to protect the environment continues.

TIMELINE
AMERICAN ENVIRONMENTAL MOVEMENT

1854 — Henry David Thoreau publishes *Walden*.

1864 — George Perkins Marsh publishes *Man and Nature*.

1889 — William Hornaday publishes *The Extermination of the American Bison*.

1890 — John Muir helps create Yosemite National Park.

1892 — John Muir and supporters found the Sierra Club.

1901 — Theodore Roosevelt begins his presidency and establishes himself as a champion of conservation.

1905 — The US Forest Service is created, with Gifford Pinchot as its head.

1911 — The North Pacific Fur Seal Treaty is approved.

1918 — The Migratory Bird Treaty Act passes.

1933 — Aldo Leopold publishes *Game Management*, the first textbook about wildlife management.

1947 — Marjory Stoneman Douglas publishes *The Everglades: River of Grass* and helps establish Everglades National Park.

1949 — Aldo Leopold's land ethic idea is explained in *A Sand County Almanac*.

1962 — Rachel Carson publishes *Silent Spring* about the dangers of pesticides.

1970 — The EPA is created, and the Clean Air Act is strengthened. The first Earth Day takes place.

1972 — The Clean Water Act is passed.

1973 — The Endangered Species Act is passed.

1989 — The *Exxon Valdez* dumps millions of gallons of oil into Alaskan waters.

1990 — The Oil Pollution Act is passed.

2010 — The worst oil spill in history occurs in the Gulf of Mexico.

2015 — Nearly 200 nations sign the Paris Climate Accord.

2017 — President Donald Trump announces withdrawal from the Paris Climate Accord.

CLIMATE CHANGE

Climate change is one of the most pressing environmental issues of modern times—and one of the most difficult to solve. As Al Gore said, *"As for why so many people still resist what the facts clearly show, I think, in part the reason is that the truth about the climate crisis is an inconvenient one that means we are going to have to change the way we live our lives."* Most of climate change is likely caused by human activity.

29

GLOSSARY

climate change: long-term change in Earth's weather patterns, caused in part by human activities such as burning oil and coal

endangered: in danger of dying out

environmental: having to do with the conditions that surround a living thing and affect the way it lives

executive order: an order that comes from the US president and must be obeyed like a law

habitat: the natural place where an animal or plant lives

inexhaustible: not capable of being used up

natural resource: something in nature that can be used by people

nonprofit: not conducted for the purpose of making a profit

pesticide: something used to kill pests, such as bugs

renewable energy: energy from sources that are naturally replenished, or renewed, such as sun and wind

technological: having to do with the practical application of specialized knowledge

wetland: land containing high levels of moisture in the soil and usually covered with water at least part of the time

FOR MORE
Information

Books

Archer, Jules. *To Save the Earth: The American Environmental Movement.* New York, NY: Sky Pony Press, 2016.

Rowell, Rebecca. *Rachel Carson Sparks the Environmental Movement.* Minneapolis, MN: Core Library, 2016.

Sonneborn, Liz. *The Environmental Movement: Protecting Our Natural Resources.* New York, NY: Chelsea House Publishers, 2008.

Websites

Environmental Movement
cosmolearning.org/topics/environmental-movement/
Read more about the environmental movement, its history, and environmental organizations here.

Environmental Movement
www-tc.pbs.org/wgbh/nova/worldbalance/roleplay/pdf/heat-env.pdf
Here's a set of instructions to guide you on getting nations to act to protect the environment!

INDEX